Leadership Begins with

Hello!

by

Diedre Windsor

© 2015 By Diedre Windsor

Copyright

Dedication

This book is dedicated to my beautiful daughter Gabrielle who kid tests and approves all of my material. I love her with everything that is me. So glad that she gets it already!

To my dear friend and staunchest supporter, Trudy L. Caldwell

And to the memory of my beloved Mom.......

Acknowledgements

My good friends who've been here for me and stayed the course from the beginning.

My colleagues for sharing their stories and best practices.

The Leaders, the Led and all who demand leadership!

Dear John,

Wishing you much success on your leadership journey!

all the best!

Diedy

Table of Contents

x

Introduction

Here's the thing. This book is not based on theory. It's not written from the perspective of academia. It's based on action. And written from a practical experience perspective intended to offer repeatable behaviors that all of us have within our grasp to incorporate into our daily routine. That's why the book is short and to the point.

I want you to do more than just read these pages. I want you to USE them! To put these practices to work in your daily life as you seek to grow and flourish as a leader.

Chapter 1

Understanding the Power in Hello!

"Hello!"

It's such a simple word really, one that's easy to say with very few letters. It's open. It's inviting. It's one of the first words we learn to say as kids. We use it to start our days, to start our conversations and even to start some of the most significant relationships in our lives.

So why won't we use it at work? What happens when we step out our front door that makes us stop looking at the people around us?

We go to work and it seems like we're all on some kind of autopilot. Its as if we step through those doors and snap on the blinders that shield us from the rest of the world. Working through our day with our heads down and our eyes closed. The goal? To make it to the end so we can grab some sleep before coming back to do it all again tomorrow.

Sound familiar to anyone?

Sometimes, especially on a pretty day, I like to sit outside during lunch and watch the people walk by. Everyone is in such a hurry! They're walking fast, eyes darting, mouths moving, as they talk into headsets and do their best to avoid interacting with anything that doesn't require a battery.

I guess that's where I'm different. I like people. I have a natural tendency to smile at others, to look them in the eye and speak to them as I make my way through the day. It doesn't matter where I am or what I'm doing. Could be the elevator in my condo, the grocery store, the post office or even as I'm simply walking down the hall at work. The setting is irrelevant. I just enjoy interacting with the people around me. It's a habit I've had forever. As a kid growing up in Detroit, it was a habit that stood out to the people around me and not necessarily in a nice way.

Thinking back I can remember my sister rolling her eyes as she told me I was "just too darn friendly!" Who knows, maybe back then I did it just to irritate her. Either way, it's how I lived my life. Over the years it's become somewhat of a deliberate habit that I purposely work into my day, and one that's served me well.

You know who has mastered the skill of seamlessly interacting with others? Kids. Kids are great at this. Take a kid to the playground and within five minutes they have found a new friend to share in their adventures. They may never see this child again, but for the next hour or so the two will become inseparable as they fight dragons, fly through space and storm the castle walls. All because someone was willing to walk up and say hello.

When I shared with a close friend the title of this book, she, like many others I'd confided in, shared a story befitting the subject. She recalled speaking with a member of her senior leadership who couldn't understand why morale was so low in their organization. He was genuinely perplexed as he called her into his office one morning to watch as the employees arrived to work.

"Look at them!" He said, shaking his head. "Why are they so unhappy?"

"Sir," she answered, knowing the answer and knowing it would shock him, "Can I speak freely and honestly?" At his nod she continued. "People are unhappy because they don't trust you. They don't know you." His jaw dropped, whether at her audacity or honesty is not entirely clear, nevertheless the conversation continued.

She explained to him that he never took the time to engage with the people around him. He gave orders rather than building consensus. Most of his day was spent in meetings and when he wasn't actually in a meeting he was hurrying to get to a meeting with his head down and his eyes locked on his ever present Blackberry, completely unaware of his surroundings.

Employees would jump out of the elevator as he approached to avoid getting caught behind closed doors with him, a leader who would not smile, would not glance their way and would not offer a greeting of any kind.

One employee regularly joked that he felt like "Mr. Cellophane." a reference to a song from the movie Chicago. The lyrics ever so fitting to the environment - "Mr. Cellophane should have been my name cause you can look right through me. Walk right by me and never know I'm there.[1]"

The conversation left the inquiring leader horrified. He had no idea his staff felt this way. It had honestly never

---

[1] "Mr. Cellophane" is a song from the movie "Chicago." Performed by actor John C. Reilly, "Mr. Cellophane" is about feeling completely ignored.

occurred to him that he was part of the problem. In his mind, he was simply busy. He was working hard and always focused on the task at hand. His next question was simple. "How do I change this?"

The answer, also simple, he must carve out time for his employees. He must make a deliberate effort to engage his staff. He started with putting the BlackBerry away – at least when he walked through the halls. He began to engage with the people around him. Knowing the hectic nature of his schedule, he made a point to arrive at the office a few minutes early each day so he could walk through the building and simply greet people as they started their day. He learned their names. He talked to them. They became more than just blank faces to walk past, they became real people. While deliberate at first, this routine became his new normal.

The result? Morale soared. People began to enjoy coming to work and the climate of the organization as a whole began to change.

And it all started with a simple, "Hello!"

This book is about the little things – the practical things that impact people and outcomes. I'll focus on those simple behaviors that tend to slip through the cracks yet make such a huge difference to people we encounter daily.

Like saying hello, an easy gesture that makes someone feel important, forms the semblance of a relationship and marks the beginning of every relationship in our lives, big or small.

That's a lot of impact from one little word.

Leadership in Action:

At the end of each chapter in this book you will find a short section titled Leadership in Action. These are simple tips designed to help you apply each new skill as you work to craft, and even change, your leadership style.

For this first chapter your challenge is simple. Take the time to interact with the world around you. Put down the BlackBerry, so to speak, and see what you can do to connect with the people you come in contact with throughout your day.

- Make Eye Contact.
- Smile.
- Say "Hello" to the people around you and see where the conversations take you.

Chapter 2

Make the Connection

Have you ever worked with or for someone, even closely, and felt that they had absolutely no idea who you were or any real details about your life?

I'm guessing the answer here is a resounding "yes!"

Now take just a moment to think back on that relationship and how it made you feel. When I ask people to describe working with this type of individual they typically come up with words like "cold," "guarded," "unfeeling," and even "robotic." Why? Because these types of connections don't make people feel valued. And when it comes to effective leadership, value is key.

Dating all the way back to my very first leadership position some two decades ago I quickly realized that understanding people, taking the time to get to know them, was critical to achieving results. It didn't matter if I was working with soldiers or civilians, people are people and they generally want and strive for the same things. Employees want leaders who care about them. They want to feel they are understood and they want to feel a connection with both their work and the people who work with them.

This is where leaders miss the boat. I've known so many different leaders in my career who focus only on results. They look at outcomes and forget to manage the journey and in doing so they lose their team. They fail to realize the importance of connecting with their team even on the most basic level.

And this could be such a simple thing! It can be as easy as knowing the name of someone's spouse or child. Or even knowing that Sasha is the cat and not the daughter. In short people are drawn to people who care. They are drawn to leaders who care.

Consider this. Several years ago I was working in an organization that faced a significant transition in the Human Resources Department. With the new leadership came the typical issues and fears that tend to come with change: fear of the unknown, a lack of knowledge around new business practices and uncertainty about the new leadership as a whole.

This change was anything and everything but seamless to the affected stakeholders. In fact, before long it felt like we were moving backwards as an organization. Although the new leadership worked hard to establish new processes, they failed horribly.

Their goal was to create greater efficiency but all they actually managed to achieve was chaos.

So where did they go wrong? Let's break it down. Without meaning to the new leadership team completely neglected one key area – employee engagement. They embarked on a host of key changes without a clear understanding of the organizational culture or the employees. They went out, sought the advice of stakeholders but failed to seek the advice of the staff to get a balanced view of the issues.

The problem stemmed straight from the top. It was evident that the new leaders had mentally dismissed the team that was in place and had essentially written them off as ineffective. The new HR Director had not made any effort to know her team. She polled stakeholders in an effort to glean where the issues were but never reconciled the information with her own staff. She acted on concerns with no input from staff and as a result morale took a thrashing and productivity plummeted. The results were catastrophic and, unfortunately it took the organization a very long time to recover. As a matter of fact, it took a change in leadership, after nine months, before real change occurred.

In this example leadership made one key misstep. They ignored the people. They made no attempt to establish an alliance with employees. They made no attempt to connect with staff, collectively or individually. They made no attempt to understand the problems from the perspective of the staff. They made no attempt to glean the strengths and weaknesses, because if they had taken the time to connect and collaborate with the staff and learned how to leverage them they might have captured and utilized the power of the team. Instead they broke a functioning unit into ineffective fragments.

Don't get me wrong, instituting change is never easy, especially if you're the new kid on the block. But, a few right steps from the beginning could definitely help achieve the desired results.

Check out the Leadership in Action for a few tips on connecting with your staff.

Leadership in Action:

- Act Fast

  When it comes to team building time is of the essence. Your team will never forget the first time you meet with them. They will be nervous, anxious and hanging on your every word. So use it to your advantage and seek to know them right from the very beginning. Be sincere and make it count. Not to be cliche' ish but, you never get a second chance to make a first impression.

- Greet the Individual, Address the Team

  When you're meeting with a new group of team members take the time to speak with each one but make sure you're offering a consistent message to the team as a whole. While you are gathering information about your new team you must ensure that your communication is clear and consistent no matter whom you are talking to.

- Put In the Time

  Spending time with your team is the best investment you can make in them. Connections take time. And time matters. So carve out the time, make the connection and commitment and watch your team thrive.

- Take Notes

  Meeting with new team members? Be ready to take some notes. After you leave take a few minutes to jot down names, job titles, family connections, pet names, sports teams and everything else you can remember from your conversations. Keep these details in a notebook and review it occasionally when needed. This will help you remember key tidbits about staff and can be helpful until you become better acquainted with your people.

Chapter 3

Listen More – Talk Less!

Most leaders love to talk. Yes, I'm including myself in that group! There, I admit it- I love to talk! And we all talk for different reasons.

Some of us talk because we believe we have something to say which those around us need to hear. Others talk because it's what they think leaders are supposed to do. And some, I'm convinced, just like the sound of their own voice.

The problem with all this talking is that it leaves out a key piece of the puzzle….listening. If you're constantly talking and ranting and making noise then when will you ever get to hear those around you?

The best advice I ever received growing up as a manager? Be still, be quiet and listen to what your team has to say. Listen with sincerity, without judgment and with the intent to learn something either from or about the person you are talking with.

Let me share what this can look like in the real world. Years ago I suddenly found myself in a brand new leadership role. I was extremely excited about the opportunity, but worried about the dangerously low morale of my team. After spending some time looking and listening I quickly found that morale was a key issue across the entire organization. This was evident not only by the habitually negative results from employee pulse surveys but it was also visibly written on the faces of the employees you passed just walking through the halls.

It was drastically apparent that something had to change if my team was going to succeed.

I took a week. One week to learn all I could about the organization as a whole before I decided to step out and try something new. After that week I started making a habit of walking the halls to meet the people who served in my division. I had a list. Every employee name in my division was on that list and my goal was to spend some quality time getting to know each and every one of them. I wanted to know more than just their name. I wanted to know them! Their work, their goals, their family, their history. It all mattered.

At first the looks I would get when I asked to talk were quite humorous. To me this was standard leadership behavior. To my team it was like I was throwing them a curve ball from way out in left field. To the point where I actually overheard two team members talking and saying that they were actively waiting for the other shoe to drop. A simple comment. One they meant as a joke, but to me it was a heartbreaking reflection of the state of the organization. Things were so polluted that my team was convinced I had ulterior motives for spending time with them. My team was so beaten down that they could not believe a member of leadership would or even could care about what they had to say.

It just made me more determined.

My next step was to create a public forum. At the end of my first month I scheduled a staff meeting where I sat and listened to the concerns of my team. Now, keep in mind that most of these individuals came to the meeting with over 20 years experience while I'm sitting on about 4 weeks. Did I value what they had to say? OF COURSE I DID! I can't buy that kind of experience, but I could surely benefit from it. All I had to do was ask. It took a few minutes to get the ball rolling but people soon began opening up and they had plenty to say. And it was sorely evident that they hadn't been given much opportunity to say it.

The success of this meeting made me more determined than ever before. From that day forward I made it a purposeful part of my day to go out into the organization and talk to people. Partly to get to know them and partly to drill into them how important they were to the big picture. These people needed to hear that their work mattered. That what they did day in and day out made a difference to the organization as a whole. I made it very clear that without them we could not succeed. I pointed out that without the Personnel team we could not attract, recruit, hire and retain valuable staff; without the Finance team we could not pay staff and procure needed services; and without the Technology team we couldn't get our work done in a timely and efficient manner. I drove home the message that without them the program staff would not be able to perform the organization's core functions. I could tell by the looks on their faces that some of the employees wanted to believe, but the others I'd have to work on.

And so I kept working. Every day. And I got results.

The tangible results came in the form of those surveys I talked about earlier. Instead of the constant stream of negative feedback we witnessed a 69% increase in employee satisfaction, on top of a measurable increase in productivity. More importantly however my team began seeking me out with new ideas and started to meet my eye with a smile when we would pass in the hall.

This change did not go unnoticed. In an environment of tight budgets, no funding, non-existent training and an ever-increasing workloads my team was thriving. They were happy in their roles and generating unmatched results. The other leaders came to me, asking what I had done differently and they were shocked by my answer.

I listened. When I, as a leader, committed to listening to those around me I instantly saw a change in how my team approached the work. Ideas began flowing through our team and there was a new level of energy I had never experienced before.

Why? Because my team felt like they mattered. They felt like their opinion mattered and that they were a valued part of the team. It was a huge difference from a very small change. All I did was listen.

Leadership in Action:

- Know your Team

  Do you know your team members? Not just their names, but really know them and what they bring to the table? You should! Take some time each day to connect with a team member. The more you learn about each team member, as well as their strengths and weaknesses, the more effectively you will be able to lead your team and help them function as a unit.

- Listen

  Even if you are the one leading the meeting it pays to sit back and actually listen to what others have to say. You've heard the saying that people are the best resource? This is only true if you are able to leverage them to their full potential. How else are you going to know what they are capable of if you don't take the time to listen to what they have to say?

- Pay Attention

  No one likes to repeat themselves. And, if you ask the same people the same questions over and over again it makes them feel as though you don't find them or what they have to say important. So focus, take notes and repeat the answers back to them. Do whatever you have to do to keep track of the details.

Chapter 4

Self-Awareness – Own Your Mess!

Right now I'd like to you take just a moment to think back. Waaaayyyyy back to the beginning of this book and to the start of our time together. One of the first stories I shared with you was about a leader who faced the reality of having to change his own behavior. He knew his employees were unhappy, but he kept missing that his own actions were the source of the tension.

The root of the problem? Self-awareness. He could see their unhappiness with the work environment, but he couldn't see how he fit into the picture.

As we go through life it is very easy to look around and point out what is wrong with everyone around us. This person is unhappy. That person is negative. She talks too much. He is too opinionated. The list truly goes on and on…..and on. But let me ask you this. When was the last time you took a detailed look at yourself? Even more, when was the last time you carefully considered how your actions and attitudes affected those around you?

The truth is that appropriate self-awareness is arguably one of the most critical character traits to develop when it comes to interacting with the world as a whole. Think about it. How can you hope to motivate, inspire and move others to action if you don't understand the impact of your actions? If you don't stop to think about this then you could quickly become the insurmountable barrier between your team and success. In fact, it all comes down to one simple statement.

~ Leadership without Awareness is Ineffective ~

So what is self-awareness? It's a very clear understanding of who you are. What are your personal and cultural values? What are your morals? What are your skills? What are your abilities? Are you full of yourself? How do you respond to stress? And how do all of these things effect those around you? Self-awareness requires stepping out of your own skin for a moment and viewing your behavior and reactions from a 3rd person perspective.

Here is the tricky part. Achieving self-awareness is a conscious choice. It doesn't tend to happen by accident. Why? Because as leaders our default tends to be on changing and guiding those around us rather than doing any serious soul searching into how we can change ourselves.

The first step? Ask for feedback and then be ready to receive it. If you are seeking a real understanding of yourself then you have to know how others truly see you. As a leader you should seek to obtain feedback from peers, subordinates and superiors alike on a regular basis. This type of approach will generate a 360-degree view of your impact. The idea is to gather data from all sources and then look for the common threads.

Let me give you a quick example. I was working with a company that was trying to increase the effectiveness of their entry-level management team. As part of my research I spent time with each of the employees who answered to this team. I asked what they liked about their position and what they wished they could change. I also asked which manager they would most like to work for.

The results were extremely interesting in that while most of the answers varied, over 90% of the employees named the same manager as the one they wanted to work for. I kept hearing over and over:

"I'm waiting for a spot to open up on Adam's team,"

or

"Adam really seems to take care of his guys."

or even

"Adam is the only manager around here who even cares."

With this kind of response my next step was to go find Adam. I needed to know what he was doing that set him so far apart from the rest of the management team. When I told him about my research and the responses I received he was actually kind of baffled. To him he wasn't doing anything special. But when I dug deep I found that he consistently asked for feedback from those around him. Asking his team, "What do you need from me?" Asking other mangers, "How can I be more effective?" He was asking for feedback and then taking the responses to heart.

The brilliance of what Adam did is that he realized he needed to be different things to different people. He was self aware enough to change his approach based on the specific person he was interacting with. To him it was a matter of asking questions and then being willing to both listen to the answers and react. It just goes to show that being an effective leader means taking a one size fits all approach and throwing it out the window.

Oh! And one more thing to keep in mind. Adam was the newest manager on the team. I say this to illustrate that effective leadership is often based on the person rather than the experience. I don't want you to feel like you need a career measured in decades to lead. All it really takes is a willingness to learn and to do the things that others won't.

Leadership in Action:

- Ask for feedback

  Make a habit of asking for feedback about your actions and habits. Get out of your comfort zone and ask someone who is not in your circle of influence.

- Accept the feedback

  Receive feedback with an open mind while being willing to filter through to find the common threads. Accept all the feedback, good and bad.

- Act on the feedback

  Be willing to change your actions based on how they affect those around you.

Chapter 5

Understand: How You Show Up Matters

What do your employees see when they see you? How do they view you? Are you considered fair? Do they call you obnoxious behind your back? Do they fear or revere you? Really think about this for a minute. How you show up greatly impacts how people respond to you and this ultimately determines your level of success – to an extent.

We've all heard the old adage that first impressions count – well, this is especially true when you're the new leader of an organization.

Employees, peers and superiors alike watch the new guy/gal like a hawk. They're looking for signs of what the future might look like. They want to know your vision, priorities, where you stand on the issues, if you're family oriented – you name it, they're curious to know. Some want to know if you're first in last out or if you have a balanced life and work normal posted hours, they want to know your thoughts on so much. It is not until after they know these things, that they can determine how to operate with you. When you show up, how you show up will give them a glimpse of what to expect. A friend of mine shared a great story that gets to the root of why this matters. In fact I'm betting many of you might have some first hand experience with what she is talking about.

Here is what she had to say:

Working in a team-based environment is always interesting. It can be amazing. It can be horrific. But it is rarely boring. It all comes down to the team and the leader. Several years ago I got to watch all of these realities unfold first hand. Luckily I was on the outside looking in.

I was working at an organization that was solely team and project based. Every team was different and each was formed with a different goal in mind. In this case my team was working on a marketing plan for a new product line. The team situated next to us was development based. They created the products, we sold them.

In this particular set-up the managers had their own office with a glass front wall. Then their respective teams were set up in cubicles or at a large table directly in front of the office visible to the manager for easy accountability. It was very much like working in a fish bowl.

Well our manager was amazing. I could go on and on about what I learned from him and habits he helped me form that still guide me to this day. But I'm not talking about him. I'm talking about the manager in the office to his right. She was a completely different story.

One day she might come in high on life and full of energy. She would be out in the cubes working with the team and cheering them on. The next? She was screaming, yelling, berating and blaming. On those days nothing was good enough. There was nothing you could say and nothing you could do but try to stay out of her way until the storm passed and she was rational again.

The problem was you never knew which side of her would show up on a given day. I always found it extremely sad that her team would gather around the coffee machine, strategically out of her line of sight, as they looked into her office and tried to gauge her mood. If they saw her smiling and waving at people who walked by they would breathe a sigh of relief and move to their own desks to start their day. If they saw her slam down the phone, they would cringe and try to figure out a way to be out of the office for the day. I even saw some of them turn around and leave, risking a write-up, just to avoid her.

The impact this had on her team was devastating. Both morale and productivity were generally low. Every time there was an opening on another team they all fought for it in an effort to get away from her and her inconsistent style of leadership.

Sound like anyone you know?

Far too many employees have been subjected to those leaders who are inconsistent. One day they might be happy and easy going and the next it is like a hurricane hit the office.

Who wants to come to work to that daily? No one. It's stressful and de-motivating.

Effective leaders realize that how you show up matters. They clearly understand that not only do your employees need to know what to expect from you, but you are responsible for setting a strong example. As leaders, you are accountable for much more than just getting the mission accomplished.

When I was a company commander in the Army my First Sergeant said to me, "Employees take on the personality of their leaders." I've found this to be true time and time again. If leaders are negative, treat people badly, show little pride in the organization – employees will follow suit. Be consistent in your behavior and the people around you will know what to expect. Exhibit behaviors that can be modeled by your staff.

As a leader you have a big responsibility. It's your job to bring everyone together, leverage their individual strengths and give them the support they need to thrive as a team member. And one of the best ways you can do that is by consistently modeling behaviors you want to see in your organization. Your actions, inactions, reactions and expectations are on full display when you show up. As a leader you must understand this and operate with this knowledge.

Leadership in Action:

- Communicate

  Employees are relying on you to communicate a clear vision, so be prepared at the onset. Be clear about your expectations.

- Show that you care

  Employees want to know that you care for them. This needs shine through in all you do. They need to know that you consider the impact to employees in your decisions.

- Set the example

  Remember, your employees are watching you. Your actions and behavior are the model. If you complain about the place, they'll complain about the place.

  Make Sense?

Chapter 6

Meet Employees Where They Are

How often have you seen a new leader come in and immediately decide that the people on board who have been doing the job for years aren't sufficient to get the mission accomplished? So many leaders believe they need people who look like them, dress like them, act like them and think like them to get the job done. They come onboard and are disappointed that their staff is not like them. Immediately, they're working to bring others just like them onboard, which doesn't necessarily make for a great team.

Having grown up in a Military environment, I learned from the onset that, from a management perspective, as far as human resources go, **you get what you get** and you make it work. Unlike the private sector where management is enabled or empowered, to a certain extent, to hire and fire at will, neither the Military, nor most Federal Government agencies, allows management the luxury. This is actually a good thing as it forces those selected to leadership positions to…well, Lead. It forces leaders to put the work in, to actually learn what motivates and inspires others to get the job done.

Experienced leaders understand they rarely get to build the "perfect" team. So they take stock of the resources they have and they learn how to leverage them. They put in the work to find out what moves and inspires those around them and then they spend the necessary time helping their team grow to its full potential.

Many years ago I had the pleasure of working with a leader who had graduated from a prestigious university with top honors (this will play in later). The staff had high hopes when he joined the organization because in addition to being extremely smart, he was equally passionate about the work of the office. Previous leaders had failed at winning over the employees largely because of their inability to successfully engage with the team. They'd heard great things about his leadership and were primed for a new start.

During his first days and weeks he spent time getting to know the staff better and understanding the mission of the organization. This was a good sign to the staff. It seemed as if they'd finally have the leader they longed for. Sadly, the honeymoon period was short lived. The new leader almost immediately began criticizing the work of the staff. He didn't hesitate to let staff know that he thought the work was 'underwhelming' and he was not shy about making it known that he was not impressed with them. Early in his tenure several (four) senior managers departed the agency – the writing was on the wall, his Mission First, People Never stance was ever so clear. Sadly, he saw nothing wrong with displaying these attitudes as he felt that a fresh perspective was needed. As if his attitude about the agency wasn't enough to bring down the morale of the staff, he hired a Senior Staff member with minimal technical expertise and no leadership experience. Wow was all I could muster daily.

This leader's fatal mistake was that he didn't take the time to understand the culture of his organization, people or programs. He didn't take the time to understand what the staff knew and how he could leverage their knowledge to strengthen his team. He shot down the work, which essentially means he shot down the employees and that didn't bode well. Members of the organization grew weary of him early and started the countdown for his replacement not long after he arrived. So they dug in and waited.....

Leadership in Action:

So, how do we meet the people where they are?

- Stop worrying about what employees don't know and figure out what they do know

  Figure out what each employee brings to the table. Learn their strengths and weaknesses and capitalize. Charge employees with assignments that will allow them to better contribute to the team effort and feel like they're a valued member of the team. At the end of the day your team does not need to look like you. They don't have to dress like you or think like you or even act like you. In fact, the diversity of thoughts and experience will only strengthen your team.

Chapter 7

Empowering your Team – The Power to Perform

In the words of that great philosopher – Elsa[2], "Let it go!"

What does it mean to empower someone? And while I realize there are several ways to answer this question, let's start with a good old fashion definition straight from the dictionary.

Here's how the Merriam Webster dictionary defines empower:

- To invest with power. Especially legal power or official authority.
- To equip or supply with ability; enable.

Sounds easy enough - right? I mean, what's hard about equipping people with what they need to do their job? Well, when you really break it down, it's not quite that simple. To truly empower someone means letting go, allowing others to make decisions and many times make mistakes. It means trusting that someone, other than yourself, can actually achieve success. After all, this is why you hire and pay staff.

I actually heard a beautiful example of empowerment from a good friend of mine named Amie. Amie was given the opportunity to take a leadership role within a new organization. She was so excited about what this company

---

[2] From Disney's Frozen

was capable of that she literally couldn't wait to walk through the door for the first time. Imagine her surprise when she found that practically every person on her team hated their job and did little more than punch the clock to get a paycheck.

She couldn't understand it! This company had so much potential! Why couldn't they just see it? So Amie did some digging. It didn't take long for her to figure out that her team was discouraged by the lack of internal promotions, training opportunities and company awards. Add to that, it was rumored that management didn't trust employees to carry out the mission of the organization. From the staff perspective they felt like they had never been given the chance to even try! This did not make for a happy or engaged bunch.

What did Amie do? She laid out a plan. Her first step was to enlist the assistance of a long-term employee to help her delve deeper into the reality of the situation they faced. She mentioned that the company had a history of failing to use their employees to their full potential. Upper management never asked for ideas or opinions and they weren't known for sharing any aspect of the decision making process. Even in the earliest stages. This left their team members feeling like drones. Like they had no purpose other than checking boxes and completing busy work, a reality that proved very frustrating, especially to the more senior staff.

So Amie decided to try a different approach. She made a point to communicate with every employee that they would have an equal opportunity when it came to promotions and other opportunities. She just had one requirement. If you wanted to be selected for advancement then you had to aid in the success of the organization. She expected every single one of her team to step up and lead when necessary.

If there was a decision to be made then she demanded not only accurate analysis but also well thought out recommendations for potential courses of action. This was required and everyone had to participate. They had to become part of the process!

Her thought was simple. "I'll provide you with the resources, remove any barriers and empower you with authority. You deliver the product that blows management away."

Her next step centered around follow-up. Amie took time every single day to talk with her employees, both giving them feedback and providing encouragement. She felt these were crucial factors to empowering and enabling them to do their very best. The result? Her team was able to achieve things they never thought possible. They were astoundingly successful. Far beyond the corporate expectation.

The lesson here? If a person, or team, is adequately empowered they have the potential to move mountains. Things they initially feel are impossible become well within their grasp. The key is they must be given the resources and authority to actually do these things. They have to be empowered.

Leadership in Action:

How do you put this into play in your daily role? Here are a few key tips.

- Treat your team members like adults.

  They are not your children and they have no desire to be micromanaged on a daily basis. Yes, this means giving up a measure of control but the long-term rewards for this action are immeasurable.

- Set realistic expectations for both yourself and your team.

  Set goals that will stretch your expectations and capabilities, but not break them. Find that fine line and learn how to walk it.

- Coach effectively my resolving issues without removing responsibility.

  Part of empowering others means being self-aware and to taking ownership of mistakes and outcomes. Failure is often a stepping-stone to success. It is how you handle that failure that will determine if the success is ever realized. Be forgiving of mistakes and use them as opportunities to both teach and learn.

Chapter 8

And the Award Goes To….. Recognizing Success and Rewarding Hard Work

Show of hands. Who here has ever felt like they worked harder than anyone else in the room….but no one noticed? Who feels like they did every single tiny thing their leader wanted, often before they asked for it, yet never received so much as a thank you?

Who just wishes someone would look them straight in the eye once in awhile and say, "Good job"?

Want to know a secret? You're not alone. In fact, I'd go so far as to say just about every person reading this book should have their hands in the air for one or all of these questions. Why? Because we all want someone to recognize our contribution. We want to know that we are doing a good job and we want someone else to notice.

Sounds simple, right? Then why is the key facet of leadership so often overlooked?

Let's look at this from a different angle. The need to feel appreciated is actually a basic human need. So important to our physical and mental well being that it is included on Maslow's Hierarchy of needs as Esteem. Maslow himself suggests that this need we have to feel appreciated and accepted is inherent. It is ingrained in us before birth to the point that it is an instinctual part of our very being.

What does it mean to be recognized? I'll tell you this - leaders often get it wrong. Many leaders immediately make the leap that recognition has to be tied to a physical reward. This is a huge mistake and it misses the very heart of the issue. The truth is that opportunities to say "thank you" or "good job" are frequent and they cost you nothing more than your time.

Simple, effective and commonly missed or taken for granted by leadership.

This is the point in the conversation where leaders tend to push back at me. Telling me, "they are only doing their job." And they're correct. Their employees are simply doing their job. But deep down inside that want leaders to acknowledge that they are doing it right. They want to know that you see them. That you recognize how hard they work and that you appreciate their efforts. Otherwise, what is it all for?

Don't get me wrong. I fully realize that there are few of us out there who would turn down recognition tied to extra bucks in our paychecks, but that's not what drives us.

For many leaders this is a learned behavior. One that they have to purposely work on and insert into their day. My challenge to you? Do it. Take the time to really look at your team and show them what you see. Tell them what they do well and your words will encourage them to do more. Ever heard the old saying that you can catch more flies with honey? It's true!

And the rewards are endless. Let me show you. Let me tell you about my wonderful friend Nicole and the story she shared with me about working on Capitol Hill for a well known Congressman.

This particular Congressman routinely made it a point to walk around and thank his staff. More so he took the time to know them as people rather than just the role they filled, to the point that he took the time to meet with each of them a few times a year just to talk about life. To learn about their family, their career goals, how they felt about their job and anything else the conversation led to. He also gave a special gift to each staffer once a year. The gift wasn't money, it had meaning. It represented something personal to that individual and it drove them to work just that much harder.

Why? Because he gave them something? No. Because he took the time to learn what mattered and offered a gift that reflected that.

Here's another hard truth. No matter what I say some of you will skip over this lesson. Sure, you'll read the words and skim through the pages but you won't see the heart of what I'm trying to share. So, with that in mind, let's take a look at the flip side. I want to show you what's at risk by sharing a story given to me by a colleague.

This particular colleague walked into my office one day visibly upset. She shared that she was losing one of her best employees and had no idea why or what she should do. She was especially hurt that the employee was simply changing jobs. There was no promotion and no increase in salary. This she could have understood. But she could not fathom what could be so horrible that would make such a valuable employee just up and leave.

My advice was that she take the time to talk with the employee and really seek to understand why they were leaving. She agreed and I'm betting you can guess what she came back with.

After their talk my colleague was right back in my office shaking her head. The employee flat out told her that she felt underappreciated. She (the employee) even pointed out that she had successfully led some major projects to completion and not once had she been thanked or acknowledged in anyway. To the employee this was an issue of culture, so they left. And at the end of that day our loss was someone else's gain.

On a more personal note, I can recall the day I was promoted to First Lieutenant in the US Army. Something happened that had a huge impact on me. Let me start off by saying that while getting promoted to First Lieutenant is significant, I should point out that it's an automatic promotion that can only be stopped if the officer has done something incredibly stupid – seriously. Again, not to minimize the significance, but promotion ceremonies at that level are not major. That said, at the time of my promotion I was stationed in the South Korean town of Kunsan. I was at a satellite base not collocated with the unit's headquarters. The leaders of the organization were stationed in the town of Suwon but lived in Seoul with their families.

For my promotion ceremony I fully expected that my Company Commander would promote me in a small ceremony at the unit. When I learned that the Battalion Commander would fly in to promote me I was kind of stunned. Mostly because the Battalion Commander was in the process of having his household goods shipped back to the United States as he was permanently changing stations. This is no small feat for the Military family. So imagine my surprise that he would break from this critical event and fly all the way to Kunsan to promote me – to First Lieutenant no less. It was humbling and it made a huge impact.

During the ceremony he said so many things about me that I didn't even think he knew. He mostly thanked me for the hard work I'd done in the unit. He said he appreciated that I stayed the course after we'd suffered major turnover. He appreciated that I extended to stay until he changed command. He talked about how he trusted me to always do the right thing which is why he's asked me to stay an extra six months in South Korea earlier that year. Admittedly, I missed some of his speech because I was so emotional by it all. His words changed me that day. I can't say it changed how I look at recognition because I really didn't have a full grasp of what it meant from a leader perspective. I would say that day his words taught me what employee recognition means.

So, hopefully by now you're wondering about ways to recognize, appreciate and acknowledge employees without a budget. I've listed a few for you in Leadership in Action. Check them out and then start a list of your own.

Leadership in Action:

- Send them a quick note (handwritten if time permits).
- Have a brown bag session for those who are setting the bar high and ask them their best practices.
- Send an email shout out to the organization about an achievement (do your homework and make sure this won't embarrass the employee).
- Go out of your way for them.

Chapter 9

Trust is Earned

Want to know everything I know about trust in one easy to remember package? Here it comes:

Trust = Easy to Break & Hard to Fix

All of the principles in this book, if followed, lead to the building of trust. Trust is the very foundation of leadership. Without it, teams fail. Without trust there are limits to a leader's ability to influence and therefore to lead.

Over the years I've been in many organizations, both Military and Civilian, and I've found the same rings true. If the members of the organization don't trust the leaders everything falls apart. Moral plummets. Productivity tanks. Basically the wheels fall off the wagon and the simplest task becomes a rapid uphill battle.

If you want your team to trust you, they need to know you are real. They need to see you act consistently and know that you mean well and want the best for them no matter the situation. They need to know that you as a leader will actively consider the people involved in every decision you make. In short, they need to know they can trust you.

Throughout my career I've seen organizations that do this well, and others that struggle and here is what I've learned. People don't leave companies. They leave people, bad leaders. And if your people can't trust you as a person, how are they ever supposed to trust you as a leader?

Let me show you what I mean.

David was a senior leader in the military. At the time of this story he was being sent to a base that was scheduled to close as a part of the military's Base Realignment and Closure (BRAC) initiative. Essentially, this meant that all of his new employees would have to make a very important decision, retire or move with the organization to a new state. Keep in mind that many of the employees had been with the organization for years and a move at that point in their lives would have had a devastating impact. Add to that the fact that the role of the new leadership team was simply to close the base.

David talked to me about the first meeting with the staff of the organization during which he asked how many employees planned to make the move. His first count was roughly 16% of the staff. This was problematic to say the very least. Trying to relocate an organization of over 5,000 members with a fraction of the manpower was not possible. It was very apparent that his first task was to find out why this number was so low.

So he did the research. He spent the time talking to his team and quickly learned that they were scared. Their main fear? How was the company supposed to survive with so few of them willing to make the move? They had the same fear he did.

David also realized that while he was focused on the move he had forgotten to focus on the people. He had not made an attempt to reach them during what had to be an extremely difficult time. He had taken over the organization with one goal in mind, close the doors. What he hadn't done was appreciate the gravity of the situation, specifically in terms of the people involved. And his actions had not created an environment of trust. The result? The employees made the decision not to relocate.

David knew it was imperative to increase the number of employees planning to relocate. The key? Winning their trust. They had to trust him if he was going to have any hope of convincing them to move half way across the country. He started by establishing bi-weekly meetings to communicate important issues regarding the move. Instead of allowing employees to speculate, to the extent possible he laid out the facts, squashed rumors and he worked on allaying the fears of those employees who were apprehensive about what was happening. Further, he sought the advice and assistance of the employees, listening to their concerns and needs helped shed some of the fear.

Over the next few months David focused on building trust. He worked on building relationships with individuals and spent extra time creating strategies designed to retain high performing employees. His efforts did not go unrewarded. At the time of the move David took 75% of the existing employees with him.

We end with trust because trust is the foundation of it all. The lynchpin, so to speak, that holds it all together.

So my challenge to you is this:

1. Start with "Hello!"
2. Build the Relationship
3. Establish Trust

And just see what happens from there. I think you might be amazed.

Made in the USA
Charleston, SC
18 December 2015